Pots,
Cans,
Cups!

Written by Clare Helen Welsh
Illustrated by Nathalie Ortega

Collins

Get the pots, Ted.

pots in the mud

I dig the mud.

Ted picks up pots.

Get the cans, Dad.

tin cans
and ducks

7

Dad tugs the can.

I pick up ten.

Dip in the net, Mum.

cups in the dock

Mum dips in the net.

pots, cans and cups

/e/

14

🐾 Review: After reading 🐾

Use your assessment from hearing the children read to choose any GPCs, words or tricky words that need additional practice.

Read 1: Decoding

- Point to the word **Get** on page 2. Ask the children to sound out and then blend the word. (*g/e/t* – **Get**)
- On pages 4 and 5, ask them to find a word that has the /u/ sound. (**mud**) Next, ask them to find the word that has the /e/ sound. (**Ted**)
- On page 7, can they find two spellings for the /c/ sound? If necessary support them by pointing to **cans** and **ducks**.
- Look at the "I spy sounds" pages (14–15). Point to the net and say: I spy an /e/ in net. Challenge the children to point to and name different things they can see containing an /e/ sound. (e.g. *nest, eggs, bench, hens, teddy, leg, wellies, cobweb, elephant, red (train), engine (on the train)*) Ask: Which words begin with /e/? (*eggs, engine, elephant*)

Read 2: Prosody

- Model reading each page with expression to the children. After you have read each page, ask the children to have a go at reading with expression.

Read 3: Comprehension

- For every question ask the children how they know the answer. Ask:
  - On page 4, why is the boy digging? (*to get the pot out the mud*)
  - On pages 8 and 9, how many cans does the boy say he has? (*ten*)
  - On pages 10 and 11, why does Mum need a net? (e.g. *because she needs to get cups out of the water*)
  - Does the text tell us that the family got lots of different things out? How do we know? (e.g. *yes, it says they got pots, cans and cups*)